TO SELF-EXCEL,

BE THE BEST VERSION OF YOURSELF!

Yolanta Lensky

Print information available on the last page

Rev. date: 03/17/2016

To order additional copies of this book, contact:
Xlibris
1-888-795-4274
www.Xlibris.com
Orders@Xlibris.com

I Poetically Ex-Ray My Life's Survey!

Dedication

To My Mother!

She is a literal reflection

Of every beacon of exception!

The light she dominates and carries

Is infinitely where my heart recovers!

Making partial use of the Sun and the stars

Warmth is all I know of my Mom's arms!

A Mother's Love is Sacred in its Display,

May Our Mothers Love Us without any Dismay!

Preface

This book is a short presentation of my creative vision and life aspirations. I have always tried to combine my imagination with a descriptive word to accomplish the sense of completion in both.

It so happened that I had miraculously survived after the memorable events of Septermber 11, 2001 that had destroyed my dreams and a successful career that had just started at Howard's Stern's show. I had to go through an ordeal of getting back to my own self afterwards. My self-discovery was a painful and unstable process that had resonated into a lot of suffering for my mother to whom, solely, I owe my soul's complete recovery. I even changed my name to be done with the past for ever.

I have also realized over time that if I don't uplift my own spirit, no one is going to do it for me, no psychiatrist, no social programs, or any medications, to say nothing about the drugs of any kind that I had used to grab at for support in my blind despair.

To soul-reside, start shining inside!

I give you a spark of mine to share it with you and to stimulate you to do the same with your loved ones and other people around you because nothing makes us happier than a smile of a person whom we helped with our kindness and compassion. I am happy with the continuation of my life that is amazingly rewarding me with invaluable bits of wisdom that I get with every consciously passing moment.

To be in a good mood, be in a hurry to do something good!

This book is my modest contribution to all those who had lost their loved ones on September 11, 2001, to the ones whose hearts are scared due to ruthless acts of violence anywhere, as well as to those who might have lost their souls in the debries of our turbulant life.

Let's Never Stop to Radiate
The Light for Everyone's Happy Fate!

Contents

Glamorize Your Life in its Entire Mass For It Too Shall Pass!

Create Your Own Center of Light,

And Be Happy and Full of Delight!

Inspiration or Desperation

Is My Life's Equation!

1. To Get a Self-Creation Inkling,

Work on Your Transformational Thinking!

2. Life is a Puzzle Quest,

Solve it with Awareness
And a Mind-Structured Zest!

Are Shaping up Our Evolutionary Function!

The Energy of the Unbreakable Spirit of Thee!

5. To Be not Destroyed by Self-Love,

Enlighten the World with the Best You Have!

6. To Be More than People Can Observe,

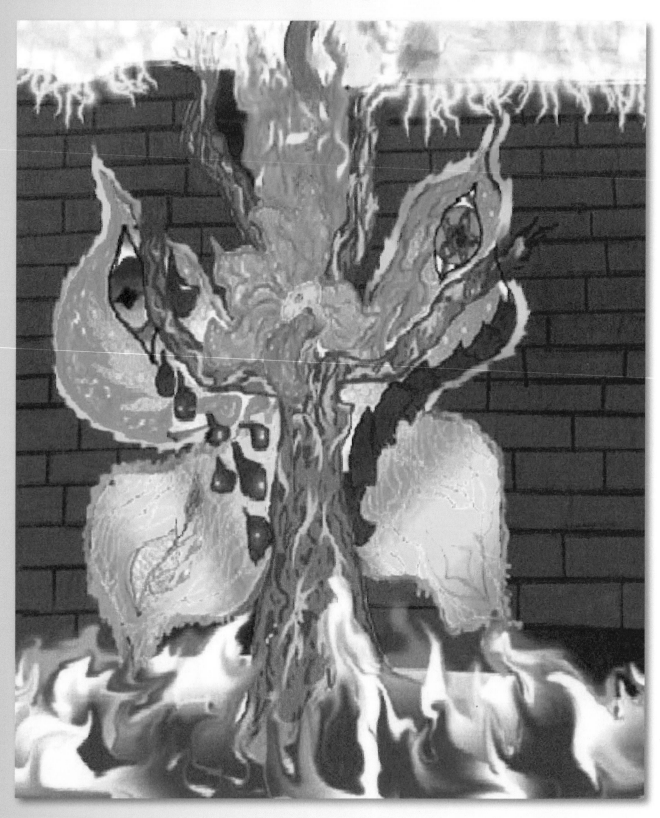

Manage Your Own Personal Surf!

7. Display Your Creative Uniqueness,

Not Commonplace Bleakness!

8. Bless Your Being with the Sun's Glee,

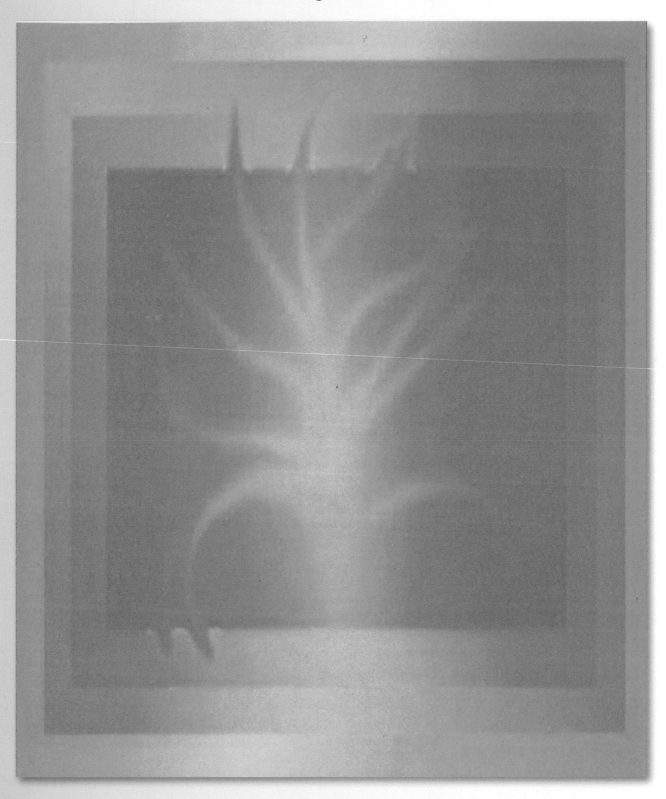

And Learn to Be Happy to Live and to Be!

9. Be Illuminated by Love in any Situation,

And Consciously Raise your Love Vibration!

10. Expand Your Inner Range - Change!

Imagination, indeed, is Infinite!

11. If You Exceed Your Emotional Volt, Learn to Timely Say,"Halt!"

Look at Life with a Wonder Glee
And Just Be!

12. Become the Artist of Your Own Framing and Reframing; Play Consciously the Life Game!

For Love of Life,
I now Implore,
For you to Set
A Candid Score!

Choreograph Your Living at Every Stage
Of Seeing, Acting, and Perceiving;
Be a Thinking Being!

13. Life is Going On,

Long Live The Belief In Life Without If!

And it's Worth Your Having Been Born!

Conclusion
"Life is a Spiral, not a Circle!"
Dr. Fred Bell

In conclusion, remember these beautiful words of Dr. Frederick Bell. Stagnation is the state we should be most afraid of. In any situation, only pushing ourselves forward can we accomplish self-realization in life. And what can be more important than managing your own life?

Also, be sure to use self-induction or self-hypnosis in the form of the boosters above, or make up your own ones. They will inevitably energize your creative powers, back up your confidence that might sag sometimes, and refresh your spirit. Be sure to remind yourself as often as you can of the boosters below:

In My Mind,
I am One of a Kind!
There wasn't, there isn't,
And there won't ever be
Anyone Like Me!

I am a Great Me;
I'm becoming the Best I could Ever Be!

About the Author

Yolanta Lensky (*former Xenia Gazarkh) is* a computer designer, a radio talk show host (*"Story in Short Pants")*, and a successful author.

The four books by Yolanta Lensky are:

1. **"Nature's Fortune"** / Leiris Publishing, 2009

2. **"Living Intelligence or the Art of Becoming!"**, *by Dr. Rimaletta Ray (Yolanta is the co-author and the designer)* / Xlibris, 2015,

3. **"Spontendor – A Flying Baby-Horse"** (Spontendor's First Adventure) *Children's book* / Xlibris, 2012

4. **"Fly Like Icarus!"** (Spontendor's Second Adventure) *Children's book* / Xlibris 2015

Email: ***yolantalensky9944@gmail.com***

Or

Rimma143@hotmail.com

Tel.(203)818-3911 cell. / 203)212-2673 / bussness/

Enrich Your Soul's
Might
Triumph is Your Birth
Right!

Printed in the United States
By Bookmasters